Illustrator:
Kathy Bruce

Editor:
Evan D. Forbes, M.S. Ed.

Editor-in-Chief:
Sharon Coan, M.S. Ed.

Art Director:
Elayne Roberts

Cover Artist:
Keith Vasconcelles

Imaging:
David Bennett

Product Manager:
Phil Garcia

Publishers:
Rachelle Cracchiolo, M.S. Ed.
Mary Dupuy Smith, M.S. Ed.

WORLD GEOGRAPHY SERIES
AUSTRALIA

BASED ON NEW NATIONAL GEOGRAPHY STANDARDS

(This series can be purchased as a complete volume or as seven separate continent books.)

Author:

Julia Jasmine, M.A.

Teacher Created Materials, Inc.
P.O. Box 1040
Huntington Beach, CA 92647
ISBN-1-55734-696-8

©1995 Teacher Created Materials, Inc.   Made in U.S.A.

The classroom teacher may reproduce copies of materials in this book for classroom use only. The reproduction of any part for an entire school or school system is strictly prohibited. No part of this publication may be transmitted, stored, or recorded in any form without written permission from the publisher.

Table of Contents

Introduction 3

Section 1: Location
- A Word or Two About Maps 6
- Where on Earth Is Australia? 9
- Where in Oceania Is_____? 14

Section 2: Place
- Islands of Oceania 15
- Look at the Map 18
- New Zealand—Australia's Neighbor to the East 19
- Physical Characteristics of Australia 20
- People in Australia 24
- Animals in Australia 26

Section 3: Relationships Within Places
- People Depend on the Environment 27
- People Adapt to and Change the Environment 29
- Technology Impacts the Environment 31

Section 4: Movement
- Movement Demonstrates Interdependence 33
- Movement Involves Linkages 35
- Movement Includes People, Ideas, and Products 37

Section 5: Regions
- The Land Time Forgot 39
- The Great Barrier Reef 44

Australian Fact Game 47

The Geography Center 52

The Culminating Activity: Making a Book 56

Glossary 71

Software Review 77

Bibliography 78

Answer Key 80

Introduction

What Has Happened to Geography?

Studies made during the last couple of decades show geography as a neglected science, even physical geography, its most traditional form. One of the suspected causes has been the higher priority of teaching subjects like math and science in the classroom. There have been many well-publicized surveys showing that people in the United States are not very well informed about the Earth they live on. Large numbers of people—including students on campuses of important universities where some of the best-publicized surveys have been conducted—were unable to identify the three largest countries on the North American continent, find Florida on a United States map, or name the oceans that border the United States on a world map. (Elementary school students love to hear about these surveys because if they are studying geography, they will be able to answer all of the questions that these college students cannot.)

During the years that the study of geography was being set aside in many of our schools in favor of other priorities, the whole focus of geography changed. Geography was once divided into two major categories: physical geography and human geography. Physical geography is concerned with the natural features of the Earth (land, water, and climate), how they relate to each other, and the living organisms, including people, on the Earth. Physical geography is divided into several categories: biogeography, climatology, geomorphology, oceanography, and soil geography. Human geography studies the patterns of human activity and how it relates to the environment around them. Human geography is divided into several categories: cultural, economic, historical, political, population, social, and urban.

It was easy to compare and contrast geography with other sciences such as astronomy, which describes the Earth in relation to its position in space, and geology, which studies the Earth's structure and composition.

Today, however, geography is crossing into other sciences, as well. We are seeing it in cultural anthropology, demographics, ecology, economics, meteorology, sociology, and zoology. Although these remain separate sciences, the lines separating them are more blurry than ever before, and many new approaches to the study of geography are being advocated.

GENIP—A National Project

In 1984, the Association of American Geographers (AAG) together with the National Council for Geographic Education (NCGE) published *Guidelines for Geographic Education: Elementary and Secondary Schools* in which they identified five fundamental themes of geography. These five themes were specifically designed and written to be used by teachers. (Crossland, 1994) In 1987, these two groups were joined by the American Geographical Society (AGS) and the National Geographic Society (NGS) to form the Geographic Education National Implementation Project (GENIP) for the purpose of implementing the aforementioned guidelines and improving the status and quality of geographic education in the United States.

Introduction (cont.)

What Has Happened to Geography? (cont.)

The Five Themes

The first theme is called *Location: Position on the Earth's Surface.* There are two kinds of locations: absolute and relative. The absolute, or exact, location of any place on Earth can be specified by giving its latitude and longitude. The relative location of a place is given by describing its relationship to other places. Absolute location is like a street address. ("I live at 2100 Oak Lane, Smalltown, CA 98765.") Relative location is a more qualitative set of directions. ("I live in the white two-story house on the corner across from the tennis courts in the park.")

The second theme is *Place: Physical and Human Characteristics.* These are the characteristics that differentiate one place from another. They include physical characteristics like landforms, bodies of water, climate, and plant and animal life, as well as land use, architecture, language, religion, type of government, and even communication and transportation if they are unique.

The third theme is *Relationships Within Places: Humans and Their Environment.* Here we ask students to take a look at the ways in which people react with their environments. This is important in this age of ecological awareness when we are trying to make good choices about the Earth.

The fourth theme is *Movement: Humans Interacting on the Earth.* This theme focuses on human interdependence. This is where a more general and comprehensive look is taken at transportation and communication.

The fifth and last theme is entitled *Regions: How They Form and Change.* GENIP defines a region as an area with one or more common characteristics or features which give it a measure of unity and make it different from the surrounding areas. The geography of the United States is often divided into a consideration of its regions—Northeast, Southeast, Midwest, Southwest, Rocky Mountain, and Pacific.

A New Mix

These themes are really a new mix of the old physical/human divisions. The first and fifth themes are more "physical" and the second and fourth more "human," while the third theme contains much of the material connected with our concern for the safety of the environment. The chief benefit of this approach may be the freshness it brings to one of the oldest of the academic disciplines. The themes themselves can be taught and discussed in any order or combination.

Introduction *(cont.)*

Australia

This book was designed to present an overview of the geography of the continent of Australia. It is divided into five sections to match the themes of the Geographic Education National Implementation Project (GENIP), an educational project backed by the nation's most prestigious geographers.

Each section contains a selection of teaching pages, maps, activities, interesting facts, review questions, and puzzles or games. A plan for using the material to construct a geography center is also included, as well as ideas for putting together a book as a culminating activity.

You will also find a glossary of the specialized vocabulary used by geographers. This will make it easier for your students to talk about the world they live in.

Location

A Word or Two About Maps

Projections

The landforms shown on maps and globes do not look exactly alike. This is because it is just as hard to "peel" a globe and flatten the Earth's "skin" out into a map as it is to peel an orange and flatten out its skin to make a smooth, even surface. Even if you can get the skin off the orange in one piece, the top and bottom edges must be broken and spread out.

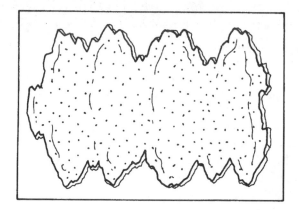

Different map makers (cartographers) have had different ideas about how to do this and have made different "projections." A projection is the way in which the map maker has chosen to flatten out the Earth's surface to make a flat map. Sometimes the map maker allows the breaks in the Earth's surface to show.

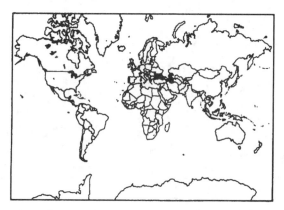

Sometimes the map maker stretches the Earth's "skin." This makes the countries near the poles look much bigger than they really are.

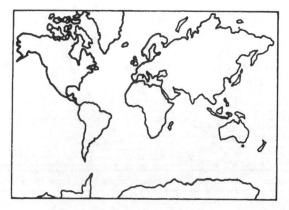

#696 Australia   ©1995 Teacher Created Materials, Inc.

Location

A Word or Two About Maps *(cont.)*

Projections *(cont.)*

Use your reference materials to find out the names of other common map projections and list them below. Research the advantages and disadvantages of each map projection you list and write them down below.

Map Projection	Advantages	Disadvantages

Location

A Word or Two About Maps *(cont.)*

The Compass Rose

The compass rose is a small drawing that shows direction on a map. Most maps show north at the top and south at the bottom, west on the left and east on the right.

Look at maps to find some different styles of compass roses and then design your own. You can shrink your drawing and make multiple copies to use on the maps you make, color, or label.

Location

Where on Earth Is Australia?

- Australia is the smallest of the seven continents.
- Australia lies in the Southern and Eastern Hemispheres between latitudes 10° S and 45° S and longitudes 110° E and 150° E.
- Australia is surrounded by the Pacific Ocean on the north, south, and east and by the Indian Ocean on the west.
- On Australia's northern side, the Great Barrier Reef extends almost to New Guinea.

Use these clues to find Australia on this map. Color it blue.

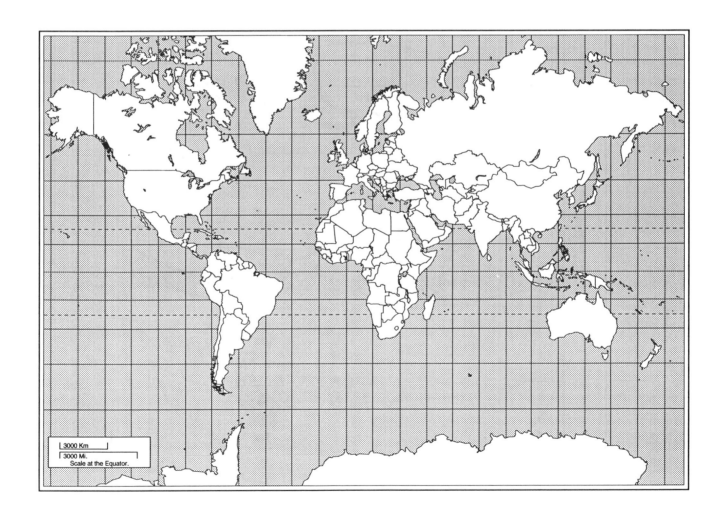

©1995 Teacher Created Materials, Inc.
#696 Australia

Location

Where on Earth Is Australia? *(cont.)*

If you think of the Earth as a ball (a sphere or globe), you can draw a line around the middle (the equator) and separate the two halves into the top half (Northern Hemisphere) and the bottom half (Southern Hemisphere). Now you can talk about something as being in the Northern or Southern Hemisphere.

More lines are drawn around the Earth parallel to the equator and evenly spaced from the equator to the North and South Poles. They are called parallels or lines of latitude. They are numbered in degrees, starting with 0° at the equator and usually spaced at 15° intervals, ending with 90° N at the North Pole and 90° S at the South Pole.

(Geographers further divide their degrees into minutes and seconds so they can be very precise in locating the position of anything on the Earth's surface.)

If you divide the Earth into its Northern and Southern Hemispheres, Australia lies entirely in the_____Hemisphere.

#696 Australia ©1995 Teacher Created Materials, Inc.

Location

Where on Earth Is Australia? *(cont.)*

You can also draw lines north and south around the Earth. These lines are called meridians or lines of longitude. They are usually shown 15° apart at the equator, but they all come together at the North and South Poles. (They also can be further divided into minutes and seconds, just like the parallels.)

The line that runs through Greenwich, England, is called the prime meridian (0°). Longitude is the distance east or west of the prime meridian. The line directly opposite the prime meridian is at 180° and is called the date line. If you are still thinking of the Earth as a ball (a sphere or globe), you can separate the two halves into the Western Hemisphere and the Eastern Hemisphere. (This is usually done along the meridians of 20° W and 160° E so all of Africa is in one hemisphere.)

If you divide the Earth into its Western and Eastern Hemisphere, Australia lies entirely in the_____Hemisphere.

©1995 Teacher Created Materials, Inc.   11   #696 Australia

Location

Where on Earth Is Australia? (cont.)

You can tell where things on the Earth are in two ways:

- You can give their exact or absolute location using latitude and longitude expressed in degrees (minutes and seconds).
- You can tell where they are in relation to other things.

Fill out the missing information to give the exact location of where you live:

house number	street name	apartment number
city	state/country	zip code

Now, use information from a map or globe to complete this description of the exact location of Australia.

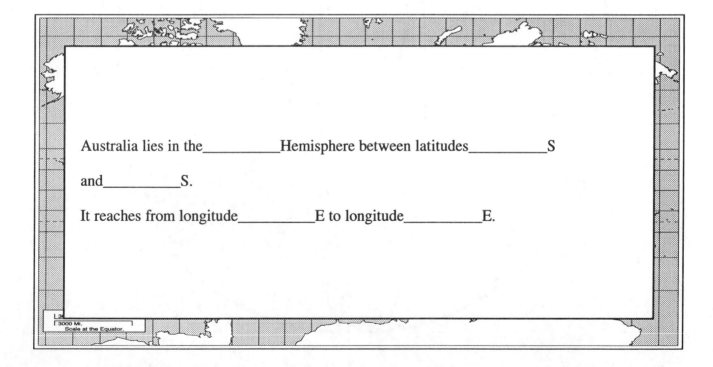

Australia lies in the _____ Hemisphere between latitudes _____ S and _____ S.

It reaches from longitude _____ E to longitude _____ E.

#696 Australia

Location

Where on Earth Is Australia? *(cont.)*

You can tell where things on the Earth are in two ways:

- You can give their exact or absolute location using latitude and longitude expressed in degrees (minutes and seconds).
- You can tell where they are in relation to other things.

Fill out the missing information to give the location of where you live in relation to other things:

I live between_____and_____

near_____

and across from_____.

Now, use information from a map or globe to complete this description of the relative location of Australia.

The continent of Australia is bordered on the north, south, and east by

the_____Ocean

and on the west by the_____Ocean.

On the northern side of Australia, the_____extends almost to the island

of_____.

©1995 Teacher Created Materials, Inc.   13   #696 Australia

Location

Where in Oceania Is _____ ?

As well as being a continent and a country, Australia is part of Oceania, the more than 25,000 islands spread across the Pacific Ocean. Use information from a globe or map, an atlas, an encyclopedia, and your geography book to write both the exact and relative locations of five of the islands in Oceania. See the next page for the names of some of these islands to choose from.

1. _____
   _____
   _____
   _____

2. _____
   _____
   _____
   _____

3. _____
   _____
   _____
   _____

4. _____
   _____
   _____
   _____

5. _____
   _____
   _____
   _____

Place

Islands of Oceania

There are 18 islands of Oceania listed below. Find them forwards, backwards, and diagonally in the word search.

```
P P H N E W C A L E D O N I A Z X L S S M V G W
T A B A G H C G V W S R N Y X V Q Z O O A A I M
D B P M W E F Q Y C K L K N D N D X L C R N L P
H T H U A A A C O O K I S L A N D S O I S U B S
Z B O N A R I S K V X P V C X N F C M E H A E Q
S B E T H N I I T V Y B S T K E G N O T A T R B
Q F N D P W E A A E K F V Z J W S Q N Y L U T P
M I I L Q G C W N N R P T M G Z T S I I L V I W
B J X V L V J K G A I I C R R E Y S S S I H S X
W I I V Z P N J V U I S S G L A F Q L L S G L B
F I S M M M P J V P I S L L N L C N A A L S A B
S S L X B F B R W P Y N L A A A X S N N A X N G
R L A C B Z S L K V T D E A N N T F D D N M D W
Q A N B M I D W A Y I S L A N D D L S S D J S N
R N D W T C H W W J Q R L G C D S S R N S T B X
J D S B V C X C A R O L I N E I S L A N D S Y T
X S T A U M O T U I S L A N D S T O N G A H G Y
Q W E R T Y U I O P A S Z X C V N B M L K J H F
A S D F G H J K L Z X V P O I U Y T R E W Q M E
J K P L C R R Y U J H G T Y J K H G F C V B O P
A B C D E F G H I J K Z G G B V C E A A S Z P U
```

Cross off the islands as you find them: Marshall Islands, Mariana Islands, Caroline Islands, Solomon Islands, Fiji Islands, Gilbert Islands, Midway Island, New Zealand, New Caledonia, Phoenix Islands, Vanuatu, Society Islands, Cook Islands, Hawaiian Islands, Tonga, Tuamotu Islands, Easter Island, Papua New Guinea

Place

Islands of Oceania (cont.)

Use information from an atlas, an encyclopedia, your geography book, or any other reference book to write two interesting facts about each island or group of islands.

1. Marshall Islands _____
   _____

2. Mariana Islands _____
   _____

3. Caroline Islands _____
   _____

4. Solomon Islands _____
   _____

5. Fiji Islands _____
   _____

6. Gilbert Islands _____
   _____

7. Midway Island _____
   _____

8. New Zealand _____
   _____

9. New Caledonia _____
   _____

Place

Islands of Oceania *(cont.)*

10. Phoenix Islands _____
_____

11. Vanuatu _____
_____

12. Society Islands _____
_____

13. Cook Islands _____
_____

14. Hawaiian Islands _____
_____

15. Tonga _____
_____

16. Tuamotu Islands _____
_____

17. Easter Island_____
_____

18. Papua New Guinea_____

Place

Look at the Map

Use the numbered list of the islands of Oceania on pages 16–17 to label the map below. Write the number of each island or group of islands on the map and use the list for a key.

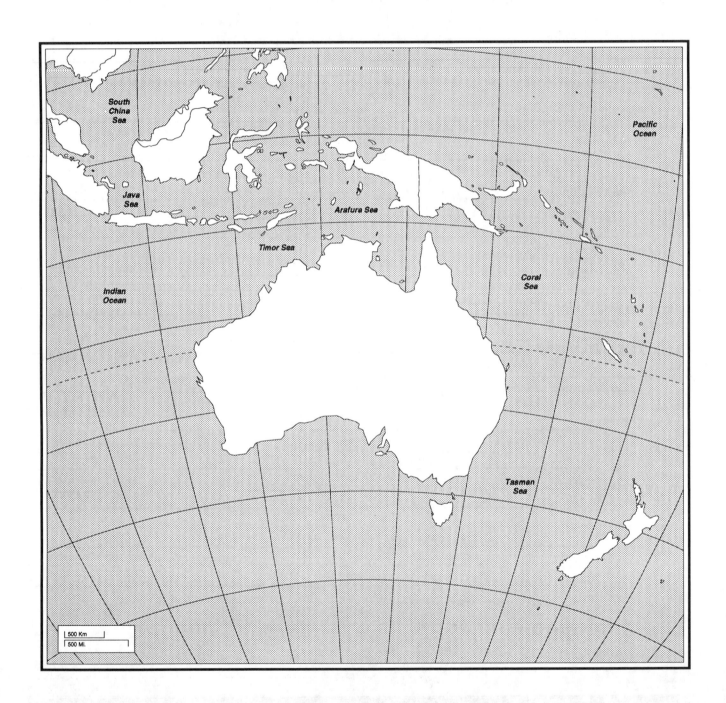

#696 Australia 18 ©1995 Teacher Created Materials, Inc.

Place

New Zealand—Australia's Neighbor to the East

Use information from an atlas, an encyclopedia, your geography book, or any other reference book to identify the places and people in or around New Zealand.

1. North Island _____

2. South Island _____

3. Tasman Sea _____

4. Lake Taupo _____

5. Cook Strait _____

6. Auckland _____

7. Wellington _____

8. Southern Alps _____

9. Mount Cook _____

10. Maori _____

Place

Physical Characteristics of Australia

Major Bodies of Water

Australia lies below the equator with the *Indian Ocean* to the west and the *Pacific Ocean* to the north and east. The *Coral Sea* lies between the Great Barrier Reef on the northeast edge of Australia and the Pacific Ocean itself, bounded by an arc of islands that consists of Papua New Guinea, the Solomons, Vanuatu, and New Caledonia. The *Tasman Sea* lies between Australia and New Zealand on the southeast side of the continent. On the south side of Australia is one of those places where two oceans come together with no particular boundary. Somewhere between Australia and Antarctica, the Pacific and Indian Oceans meet and blend.

Use reference sources to label these major bodies of water on the map of Australia.

Place

Physical Characteristics of Australia *(cont.)*

Mountains, Plains, and Reefs

Australia is an ancient continent. Its highlands have been worn down through the ages. Its highest mountain range, the *Great Dividing Range,* runs the length of the east coast. The highest peak of that range, *Mount Kosciusko,* reaches an altitude of only 7,310 feet (2,217 m). To the west of these mountains, there is an area where wheat is grown. As the air from the Pacific rises over the mountains and deposits its moisture in the form of rain, the water sinks into the ground, forming The *Great Artesian Basin.* About a third of Australia depends on artesian wells for its water supply. The great plains and deserts of central and western Australia lie beyond. This is a land of dust, blazing heat, and little vegetation. Australians call it the *outback.* It is divided on the map into areas such as the *Great Sandy Desert,* the *Great Victoria Desert,* and the *Tatami Desert.* In the outback, and almost exactly in the middle of Australia, is *Ayers Rock,* which is 1,000 feet (303 m) high. In contrast to this hot dry area, one of Australia's most impressive features is the *Great Barrier Reef.* It lies along the Queensland coast in the Coral Sea. It is 1,250 miles (2,000 km) long, the longest reef in the world.

Use reference sources to label these physical characteristics on the map of Australia.

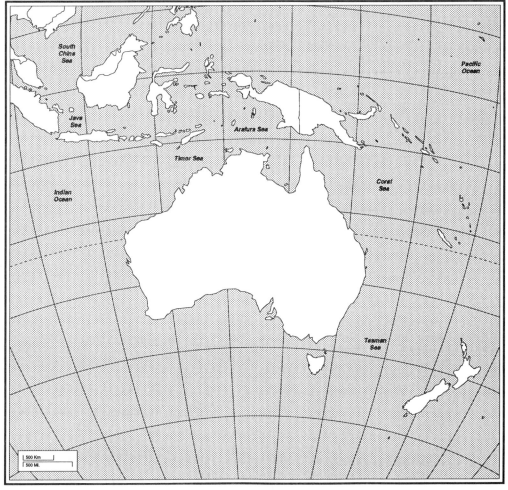

Place

Physical Characteristics of Australia *(cont.)*

Other Bodies of Water

Australia's rivers have a hard time in the hot, dry outback. On many maps, they are drawn with dotted lines. Some of the lakes are drawn that way too. The *Murray River* and its branches form Australia's largest river system. The *Darling River,* Australia's longest, feeds into the Murray River.

Many of Australia's bodies of water occur around the edges of the continent. The large inward dip in Australia's south coast is called the *Great Australian Bight,* and the narrow body of water separating the island of Tasmania from the mainland is called *Bass Strait.*

Use reference sources to draw in the rivers and lakes on the map on the next page. Then label the bodies of water with their numbers and use the list for a key.

---

1. Lake Mackay
2. Lake Disappointment
3. Lake Carnegie
4. Darling River
5. Murray River
6. Lachlan River
7. Ashburton River
8. Fitzroy River
9. Victoria River
10. Arafura Sea
11. Gulf of Carpentaria
12. Timor Sea
13. Spencer Gulf
14. Shark Bay
15. Great Australian Bight
16. Bass Strait

Bonus Questions!

What does it mean when lakes and rivers are drawn on a map with dotted lines?

_____

_____

Which important line of latitude runs through the middle of Australia?

_____

_____

Place

Physical Characteristics of Australia (cont.)

Other Bodies of Water

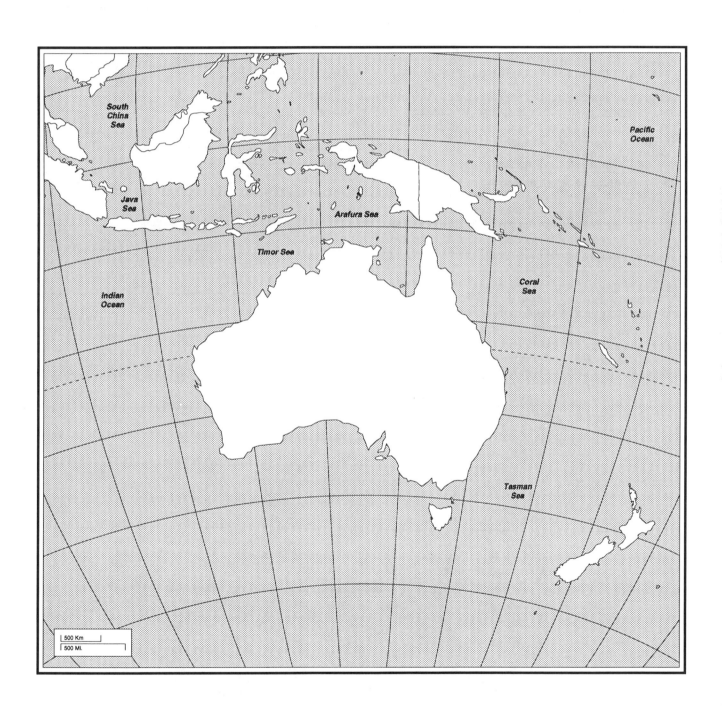

Place

People in Australia

Australia was first discovered and settled by the people who are now called the aborigines. They probably came from Asia by way of what is now Indonesia about 40,000 years ago.

Australia was claimed for England by Captain Cook who discovered it in 1770. For a long time it was used as a penal colony, a place to send convicts. Then it became a destination for adventurous people who went to seek their fortunes. It remained a colony of Great Britain until 1901, when it became an independent country. Australia is now a self-governing member of the British Commonwealth and is going through a period of growing nationalism.

Almost all of the people of Australia live in cities and towns along the southeast coast. A few people who farm the land live on the eastern edge of the outback. Historically the aborigines lived in the outback, where they developed a way of dealing with the harsh environment. Today, many of them have moved to cities and towns, where they live in almost complete poverty.

Australia the continent and Australia the country fill up the same land area. The country is divided into six states and two federal territories. List these states and territories below and label them on the political map of Australia.

_____   _____

_____   _____

_____   _____

_____   _____

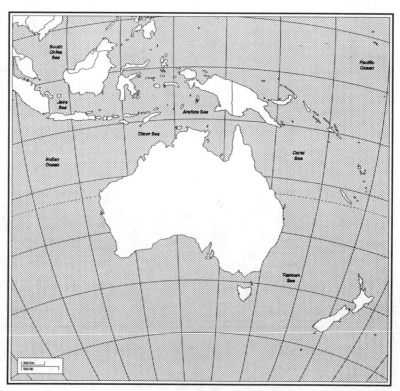

Place

People in Australia *(cont.)*

The Aborigines

The Australian aborigines developed a way of life that allowed them to survive in the outback. Although they live in a very primitive manner, they have complex and interesting social and religious customs. Some of the problems that Australia is facing today have to do with tourists visiting sacred places of the aborigines. See what you can find out about these people.

Survival Skills

_____
_____
_____
_____
_____

Sacred Places

_____
_____
_____
_____
_____

Similarity to Native Americans

_____
_____
_____
_____
_____

Place

Animals in Australia

Read the clues and unscramble these words related to the Australian animals.

1. _____ an animal that carries its young in a pouch (rampuslia)
2. _____ a marsupial that looks like a teddy bear (loaka)
3. _____ the tree that provides for food and shelter for the koala (calypteus)
4. _____ an animal that hops on two strong back legs (nogakroa)
5. _____ a small kangaroo-like marsupial (ballway)
6. _____ a thick, burrowing marsupial that lives on the island of Tasmania (mobtaw)
7. _____ an unusual mammal living in the waters around Australia (godung)
8. _____ an egg-laying mammal with webbed feet and a bill like a duck (spytalup)
9. _____ a large flightless bird that looks like an ostrich; related to the cassowary (mue)
10. _____ an egg-laying mammal that is also called the spiny anteater (andchie)
11. _____ a kind of lizard (kniks)
12. _____ the Australian wild dog (doing)
13. _____ a large flightless bird that looks like an ostrich; related to the emu (sowcarsay)
14. _____ a bird with a cry like a laughing donkey (burakokoar)
15. _____ small marsupials with long narrow noses and tails like rats (candiboots)
16. _____ a bird with a beautiful lyre-shaped tail (dribelry)
17. _____ ferocious and ugly little animal that is native to Tasmania (sTanmania viled)
18. _____ a bird that uses vines to "stitch" its nest together (dribvarwee)

#696 Australia 26 ©1995 Teacher Created Materials, Inc.

Relationships

People Depend on the Environment

Make a list of Australia's natural resources.

_____
_____
_____
_____
_____

Then create a symbol to go with each natural resource and make a key. Using your newly created symbols, show these resources on the map of Australia on the next page.

Resource Key

Relationships

People Depend on the Environment (cont.)

Resource Map

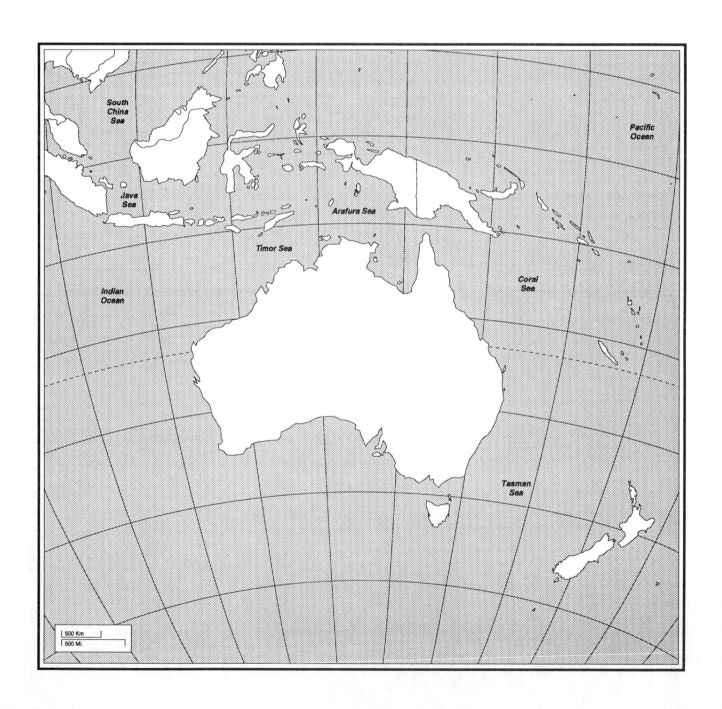

Relationships

People Adapt to and Change the Environment

People adapt to and change the environment in many ways. Think of some possible solutions that may solve these environmental problems:

Very dry conditions for farming:

_____
_____
_____
_____

Hills too steep for crops:

_____
_____
_____
_____

Areas that flood:

_____
_____
_____
_____

Housing in hot climates:

_____
_____
_____
_____

Relationships

People Adapt to and Change the Environment *(cont.)*

People adapt to and change the environment in many ways. Think of some possible solutions that may solve these environmental problems:

Housing in cold climates:

_____
_____
_____
_____

Clothing in hot climates:

_____
_____
_____
_____

Clothing in cold climates:

_____
_____
_____
_____

Transportation in mountainous or hilly areas:

_____
_____
_____
_____

Relationships

Technology Impacts the Environment

Resources are things that are valued and used by people. Natural resources are the resources that occur in nature, such as minerals in the Earth, trees, water, and air.

The way people feel about and use natural resource changes as new technologies are developed.

Research how the use of natural resources has already changed in Australia and how it may change in the future.

Type of Resource	Past	Present	Future
Fuel for heating			
Fuel for ships			
Fuel for trains			
Fuel for cars			

©1995 Teacher Created Materials, Inc. #696 Australia

Relationships

Technology Impacts the Environment *(cont.)*

Type of Resource	Past	Present	Future
Materials for building			
Materials for containers			
Propellant for spray cans			
Material for paper			
Treatment of the air			
Use of water			

Movement

Movement Demonstrates Interdependence

Why do human activities require movement? _____
_____
_____

Do the people in your family go places? _____ Choose two people and answer the following questions:

	Person #1	Person #2
Who?		
When?		
Where?		
How far?		
How often?		
Why?		
Mode of transportation?		

©1995 Teacher Created Materials, Inc.

Movement Demonstrates Interdependence *(cont.)*

Use reference sources to figure the distances between these Australian cities, as well as between Australian cities and cities in other countries around the world.

Melbourne/Sydney _____

Sydney/Brisbane _____

Canberra/Perth _____

Melbourne/Wellington, New Zealand _____

Sydney/Tokyo _____

Sydney/Manilla _____

Melbourne/Honolulu _____

Melbourne/Mexico City _____

Perth/Rome _____

Melbourne/Miami _____

Sydney/London _____

Brisbane/Hong Kong _____

Signpost:
- Melbourne 3125 km
- Perth 2600 km
- Sydney 3110 km
- Brisbane 2930 km

Movement

Movement Involves Linkages

List some of the ways people traveled from place to place in Australia in the past.

___

List some of the ways people travel from place to place in Australia in the present.

___

Bonus Question!

Why did methods of transportation change?

___

Movement Involves Linkages *(cont.)*

Movement

How will people travel around Australia in the future?

_____
_____
_____
_____

Design your own future method of transportation. Explain it and then draw a picture of it below.

_____
_____
_____
_____

This Is How My Future Transportation Will Work:

_____
_____
_____

This Is How My Future Transportation Will Look:

#696 Australia   36   ©1995 Teacher Created Materials, Inc.

Movement

Movement Includes People, Ideas, and Products

People go places for business and for pleasure. Going somewhere for pleasure is called touring.

Where have you gone for pleasure?

___

Where would you like to go?

___

Ideas can travel too. List some of the different ways ideas travel from place to place.

___

Products also travel. What are some of the ways products travel?

___

Movement

Movement Includes People, Ideas, and Products *(cont.)*

Think about one of the places you would like to visit in Australia. Design a cover for a travel brochure about that place. Sketch your design below. Write a description of the place that will make other people want to travel there too.

_____
_____
_____
_____

Regions

The Land Time Forgot

Australia as a Region

A region is a portion of the Earth's surface that has characteristics unlike any other. The whole continent of Australia is itself a region. Its age has allowed the mountains to weather. Its isolation has given it unusual animals. Its physical features and climate have made life very different for both its native people and its current population.

The weather is hot, dry, and dusty. Water is scarce, but is attainable from artesian wells. These wells are used for watering sheep and cattle, which makes possible enormous sheep and cattle ranches.

Use reference books to find out about artesian wells. What are they? How do they work? Write about them below.

_____

_____

_____

_____

_____

_____

Children go to school, no matter where they live. How do they go to school in the outback?
Use reference books to find out about education in different parts of Australia. Write about it below.

_____

_____

_____

_____

_____

_____

_____

_____

©1995 Teacher Created Materials, Inc.   #696 Australia

Regions

The Land Time Forgot *(cont.)*

The Aborigines Across the Curriculum

The word "aborigines" was formerly used to refer to the original people of any geographical area. Now, however, *aborigines* are understood to be the native people of Australia, and the word is restricted by scientists to that usage. The aborigines live in the Australian *outback*, where they maintain a delicate balance with their environment. They trap rare rainfall by building little dams, and they carry water in the shells of huge eggs laid by the *emu* and the *cassowary*, birds of the outback that look like ostriches. They invented the weapon known as the *boomerang* and use it for hunting today but used it also for warfare in the past. *Ayers Rock* in the *Northern Territory* is one of their most sacred places.

1. **The Aborigines**
   Be ready to report on the aborigines. Find out what these people hunt, if they migrated, what their family groups are like, and how they live today. Write down any other facts that you think are interesting.

   _____
   _____
   _____
   _____
   _____

2. **The Outback**
   Write a poem about the outback. This is a wild and harsh environment, but it is also full of color and excitement. Try to see a video tape or read an illustrated book about this interesting place before you write your poem.

   _____
   _____
   _____
   _____
   _____

Regions

The Land Time Forgot *(cont.)*

The Aborigines Across the Curriculum *(cont.)*

3. Put the italicized terms on page 40 in ABC order and tell how many syllables are in each of them.

4. **The Boomerang**

Find out as much as you can about this weapon. Write your findings on the lines below. (Hint: There are two kinds.)

_____

_____

_____

_____

_____

_____

_____

_____

The Land Time Forgot (cont.)

The Aborigines Across the Curriculum (cont.)

5. Ayers Rock

Ayers Rock is a sacred place to the aborigines. Read about some places that people have thought were sacred. Make up a story explaining how Ayers Rock became a sacred place. Call your story "The Biggest Rock on Earth."

___
___
___
___
___
___
___
___
___
___
___
___
___
___
___
___
___
___
___
___
___
___
___
___

Regions

The Land Time Forgot (cont.)

The Aborigines Across the Curriculum (cont.)

6. Scientists

What kind of scientists study people like the aborigines? What else do they study? How do they learn to be this kind of scientist? See what you can find out about these scientists.

_____

_____

_____

_____

7. Emu/Cassowary/Ostrich

These three birds are very much alike. Make a chart to compare their characteristics. Keep track of your facts here as you do your research.

	Emu	Cassowary	Ostrich
Country			
Height			
Weight			
Size of egg			
Unusual habits			

Regions

The Great Barrier Reef

The Great Barrier Reef is the longest reef in the world. People go from all over the world to snorkel and scuba dive there. It is home to many varieties of sea life, both plants and animals.

Find information about the Great Barrier Reef in reference books and answer these questions.

1. What is a reef?

   _____

2. How long is the Great Barrier Reef?

   _____

3. Where is it located?

   _____

4. How was it built?

   _____

5. How long did it take?

   _____

6. How many species of fish live on the Great Barrier Reef?

   _____

Regions

The Great Barrier Reef *(cont.)*

7. How many kinds of coral live there?

   _____

8. Name four kinds of coral that live on the Great Barrier Reef.

   _____

   _____

   _____

   _____

9. How far is the Great Barrier Reef from the shore?

   _____

10. What are some reasons the Great Barrier Reef is in trouble?

    _____

    _____

    _____

    _____

    _____

    _____

    _____

The Great Barrier Reef *(cont.)*

Meet with a partner or group to brainstorm ideas for helping to save the Great Barrier Reef. List your ideas below.

_____
_____
_____
_____
_____

Decide on the best of your ideas and formulate a plan for putting your idea into action. List the steps of your plan below.

1. _____
   _____
   _____

2. _____
   _____
   _____

3. _____
   _____
   _____

4. _____
   _____
   _____

5. _____
   _____
   _____

Australian Fact Game

This game can be played in different ways:

Game 1—You can use a Jeopardy format. Students love this, and they can set it up all by themselves or with just a little help. Run the answer cards on one color of paper and the question cards on another color for easy sorting.

Game 2—You can make a card game like rummy. All the cards should be run on one color for this. Shuffle the cards and deal five to each player. Put the leftovers facedown or in the middle of the table. Players draw from the stack and discard in another stack. The object of the game is to lay down pairs by matching questions and answers. You can make it more complicated by allowing students to challenge one another's matched pairs if they think the matches are incorrect. Have students keep track of the rules they make and write game directions.

Fact Game Cards

It is the smallest continent in the world.	What is Australia?
It is a weapon used in hunting.	What is a boomerang?
It is the only continent that is only one country.	What is Australia?

©1995 Teacher Created Materials, Inc.   #696 Australia

Australian Fact Game (cont.)

Fact Game Cards (cont.)

This area is called the "outback."	What are the huge deserts and plains?
This is known as the land "down under."	What is Australia?
This is the largest and most well-known rock in the outback.	What is Ayers Rock?
It is the largest coral reef in the world.	What is the Great Barrier Reef?
It is a large island off the southeast end of Australia.	What is Tasmania?
They are the native people of Australia.	Who are the aborigines?

Australian Fact Game (cont.)

Fact Game Cards (cont.)

These animals have pouches in which they carry their babies.	What are marsupials?
It lives in eucalyptus trees and looks like a teddy bear.	What is a koala?
It jumps along with the help of strong back legs and a heavy tail.	What is a kangaroo?
It is a bird that looks a lot like an ostrich.	What is an emu?
It is the capital city of Australia.	What is Canberra?
It is the capital city of New Zealand.	What is Wellington?

©1995 Teacher Created Materials, Inc.   49   #696 Australia

Australian Fact Game (cont.)

Fact Game Cards (cont.)

This is the official language of Australia.	What is English?
This is the wild dog of the outback.	What is the dingo?
This is the name given to the huge sheep and cattle ranches of the outback.	What are stations?
This is the longest and highest chain of mountains in Australia.	What is the Great Dividing Range?
This body of water separates Tasmania from the main continent.	What is Bass Strait?
Australis is the Latin word for southern.	From what word does Australia get its name?

Australian Fact Game (cont.)

Fact Game Cards (cont.)

Let your students make their own question-and-answer fact cards. Students usually like to make extra hard ones in hopes of stumping each other, so have them write the book and page number where the information can be found on the question card.

	Book:_____
	Page: _____
	Book:_____
	Page: _____
	Book:_____
	Page: _____
	Book:_____
	Page: _____
	Book:_____
	Page: _____

The Geography Center

Putting the Center Together

You can set up your Geography Center in a corner of your classroom and make it as simple or as elaborate as you want. The center should have a map, a globe, and an atlas. (Several maps, a couple of globes, and multiple copies of the atlas would be even better.) A table and chairs will facilitate group activities and discussions. A supply of writing and drawing materials will also come in handy. A bookcase, shelf, or window sill can be utilized for storing reference books. The more reference books you can provide, the better the assigned projects will be. If you have access to a TV, VCR, and tapes, you can show movies about the places you are studying. There are many tapes of this variety available, and the visual learners in your class will really appreciate this. Cushions for sitting on the floor to read or view tapes add a cozy touch.

Making the Center Work

You can make the Geography Center part of your instructional day by scheduling groups to do center work. Change the materials daily or weekly or provide a set of task cards at the beginning of the unit and expect each student to work through them individually or as part of a group. (See pages 53–55.)

Use Portfolios

Have students make portfolios and store them in containers in an accessible area of your center. Try using the inexpensive but sturdy plastic crates that are available at local hardware stores. Make students responsible for their own progress by having them file their own work, both completed work and work in progress. Have students create attractive covers for their portfolios so the accumulated work can be attractively displayed at your school's open house.

Deck the Walls

Encourage artwork, creative writing, and exploratory math to go along with your geography unit and spread it throughout the curriculum. Display these products on a bulletin board in your Geography Center. Have students mount and post their own work. They can cut out letters and create colorful captions for the board.

Have another bulletin board reserved for posting newspaper and magazine articles dealing with the continent you are studying. Encourage your students to bring in these articles, share them, and discuss their meaning and importance.

The Geography Center (cont.)

Task Cards

Task Card #1

What is the longest river on the continent?

How long is it?

Through which state/territory or states/territories does it flow?

Task Card #2

What is the most important mountain range on the continent?

How long is it?

In which state/territory or states/territories are these mountains found?

Task Card #3

What is the highest mountain peak on the continent?

How tall is it?

In which state/territory is it found?

Task Card #4

What is the largest state/territory on the continent?

What states/territories or bodies of water border it?

What is its capital city?

©1995 Teacher Created Materials, Inc. 53 #696 Australia

The Geography Center (cont.)

Task Cards (cont.)

Task Card #7
What animals are associated with the continent?

In what state/territory or states/territories do they live?

Are they in any danger in today's civilization?

Task Card #8
What variations in climate are found on the continent?

What variations in weather are found on the continent?

Can people live in all parts of the continent?

Task Card #5
What is the smallest state/territory on the continent?

What states/territories or bodies of water border it?

What is its capital city?

Task Card #6
What is the largest lake on the continent?

In which state/territory or states/territories is it found?

Which river is associated with it?

#696 Australia ©1995 Teacher Created Materials, Inc.

The Geography Center *(cont.)*

Task Card Response

Leave a stack of these task card response forms in the geography center for students to use.

Name _____ Date _____

Task Card # _____

Question #1

_____

_____

_____

_____

Question #2

_____

_____

_____

_____

Question #3

_____

_____

_____

_____

Bonus

I also learned _____

_____

_____

_____

The Culminating Activity: Making a Book

Method
You and your students can go about bookmaking in many different ways. Here are some suggestions:

- The book can be your students' showcase portfolios.
- Students can review and reflect upon the work they have accumulated in their portfolios, select the most representative samples or the pieces they like best, and put these things together in book form.
- The book can be a showcase portfolio based on the teacher's criteria.
- Have students select work from their portfolios based on a list you develop.
- The book can be comprised of new material that sums up the unit.
- Have students complete various assignments meant specifically for inclusion in their books, showing their grasp of the material. (See pages 57–67.)

Contents
In most cases you will probably want your students to include maps, facts about both physical and political geography, research about animals, people, and resources. They can review or report on any books they have read about the continent, and they can write about what they have learned and how it has affected the way they view the world.

Cover
You can specify and provide the design for the cover so that all of the books will be uniform, or you can encourage your students to design a cover that is representative of the continent. A collage of pictures cut from magazines and travel brochures is an option that works well.

Be sure to laminate the finished covers so the books can be used as part of your classroom library or Geography Center reference shelf. Your students may also want to share their books with students in other classes.

Exciting ideas for binding and publishing follow on pages 68–70.

The Culminating Activity: Making a Book (cont.)

Trace an outline map of the continent. Transfer information about its physical features from all of the maps you have made. You might want to use different colors to create a key.

Name _____ Date_____

Map of Physical Features

The Culminating Activity: Making a Book *(cont.)*

Use the information you have already gathered or do some new research to complete this page.

Name _____ Date_____

Facts About Physical Features

Area: _____
_____

Highest Point: _____
_____

Lowest Point: _____
_____

Largest Island:_____
_____

Longest River:_____
_____

Largest Lake: _____
_____

Tallest Waterfall:_____
_____

Largest Desert: _____
_____

Longest Reef: _____
_____

The Culminating Activity: Making a Book (cont.)

Trace an outline map of the continent. Transfer information about its political features from all of the maps you have made. You might want to use a numbered list to create a key.

Name _____ Date _____

Map of Political Features

The Culminating Activity: Making a Book (cont.)

Use the information you have already gathered or do some new research to complete this page.

Name _____ Date _____

Facts About Political Features

Population: _____

Largest State/Territory (by area): _____

Largest State/Territory (by population): _____

Smallest State/Territory (by area): _____

Smallest State/Territory (by population): _____

Largest Metropolitan Area (by population): _____

_____

_____

_____

_____

Newest States/Territories: _____

_____

_____

_____

_____

The Culminating Activity: Making a Book (cont.)

Use the information you have already gathered or do some new research to complete this page.

Name _____ Date_____

The People

The people of this continent belong to these ethnic groups:

_____
_____
_____

They speak these languages:

_____
_____
_____

They live in these different environments:

_____
_____
_____

Their ways of life have changed or are changing:

_____
_____
_____
_____

The Culminating Activity: Making a Book (cont.)

Pick the city on the continent that is most interesting to you. Use the information you have already gathered or do some new research to complete this page.

Name _____ Date _____

The city of _____.

This city is in _____

Area: _____

Population: _____
_____

Language(s): _____
_____

Ethnic Groups: _____
_____

Religious Groups: _____
_____

Famous Natural Features: _____
_____
_____

Famous Constructed Features: _____
_____
_____
_____
_____

#696 Australia 62 ©1995 Teacher Created Materials, Inc.

The Culminating Activity: Making a Book *(cont.)*

Use the information you have already gathered or do some new research to complete this page.

Name _____ Date _____

The Animals

The best known animals of this continent are _____
_____
_____

The animals of this continent are important because _____
_____
_____

The animals that still live in their natural habitats are _____
_____
_____

The animals that are on the endangered list are _____
_____
_____
_____

They are on the endangered list because _____
_____
_____
_____
_____

©1995 Teacher Created Materials, Inc.   63   #696 Australia

The Culminating Activity: Making a Book (cont.)

Keep track of the books you read about the continent on this log.

Name _____ Date _____

Book Log

Title: _____	Fiction: _____
Author: _____	Nonfiction: _____
Illustrator: _____	Rating: _____

Title: _____	Fiction: _____
Author: _____	Nonfiction: _____
Illustrator: _____	Rating: _____

Title: _____	Fiction: _____
Author: _____	Nonfiction: _____
Illustrator: _____	Rating: _____

Title: _____	Fiction: _____
Author: _____	Nonfiction: _____
Illustrator: _____	Rating: _____

#696 Australia   ©1995 Teacher Created Materials, Inc.

The Culminating Activity: Making a Book (cont.)

Use copies of this form to review your favorite nonfiction books about the continent you have been studying.

Name _____ Date _____

Book Review/Nonfiction

Title: _____

Author: _____

Illustrator: _____

Summary: _____

_____

_____

_____

_____

_____

Reasons I liked or did not like this book: _____

_____

_____

_____

_____

_____

_____

Bonus!

If you liked this book and think other people should read it, you can do one of two things. (1) Write a paragraph or two telling how a nonfiction book can help you understand a continent or a country and post it on the bulletin board in the Geography Center. (2) Make a poster advertising the book and post it on the bulletin board in the Geography Center.

The Culminating Activity: Making a Book (cont.)

Use copies of this form to review your favorite fiction books about the continent you have been studying.

Name _____ Date _____

Book Review/Fiction

Title: _____

Author: _____

Illustrator: _____

Summary: _____

_____

_____

_____

_____

_____

_____

Reasons I liked or did not like this book: _____

_____

_____

_____

_____

_____

_____

Bonus!

If you liked this book and think other people should read it, you can do one of two things. (1) Write a paragraph or two telling how a fiction book can help you understand a continent or a country and post it on the bulletin board in the Geography Center. (2) Make a poster advertising the book and post it on the bulletin board in the Geography Center.

The Culminating Activity: Making a Book *(cont.)*

Write a reflective essay in which you discuss the ways that studying geography has given you a better understanding of the world and the people in it.

Name _____ Date _____

Title: _____

The Culminating Activity: Making a Book (cont.)

Book Binding Ideas

1. Stack all the pages of the book in a neat pile.

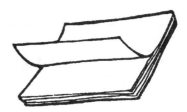

2. Place a blank sheet of paper on the top and bottom of the pages.

3. Leaving approximately 1/2" (1.25 cm) border, staple or sew all of the pages together on the left side.

4. Place two pieces of lightweight cardboard side by side. (Cereal boxes work well.) Each piece should be 1/2 to 1" (1.25 to 2.5 cm) larger than the size of the pages in the book.

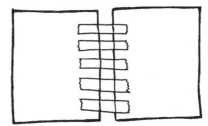

5. Leaving approximately 1" (2.5 cm) between them, tape the cardboard pieces together.

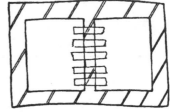

6. Put the cardboard on top of your covering material (e.g., fabric, wallpaper, contact paper, or wrapping paper). Glue the cardboard and covering material together, leaving a 1 to 1 1/2" (2.5 to 3.25 cm) material border.

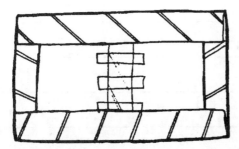

7. Fold up the edges of material over the cardboard and glue in place.

8. Glue the blank pages to the inside of the cardboard covers. Your book is ready to read and share.

The Culminating Activity: Making a Book (cont.)

Pop-Up Books

1. Fold a 8 1/2" x 11" (22 cm x 28 cm) piece of paper in half crosswise.

2. Measure and mark 2 3/4" (7 cm) from each side along the fold. Cut 2 3/4" (7 cm) slits at the marks.

3. Push cut area inside-out and crease to form the pop-up section.

4. Draw, color, and cut out the object to get "popped-up."

5. Glue it onto the pop-up section.

6. Glue two pages back to back, making sure the pop-up section is free.

7. Glue additional pages together, making as many pages (including pop-up pages) as you like. Be sure to include a free sheet on both the front and back so that those pages can be glued to a cover.

8. Glue a cover over the entire book.

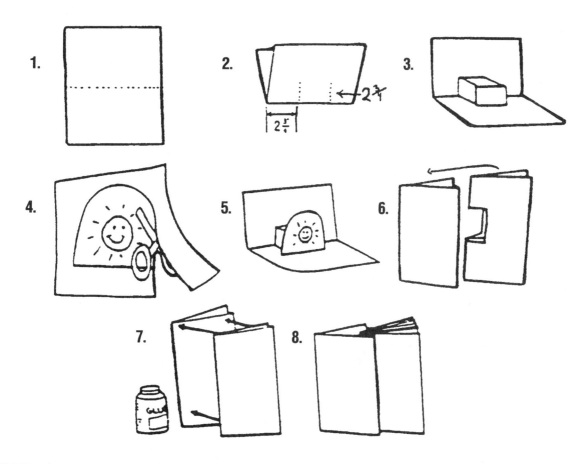

©1995 Teacher Created Materials, Inc.

The Culminating Activity: Making a Book (cont.)

Real Markets for Student Writing

Student writing can be sent to the following addresses. Check your professional journals for more sources.

Children's Playmate (ages 5–8)
P.O. Box 567B
Indianapolis, Indiana 46206

Cricket (ages 6–12)
Cricket League
P.O. Box 300
Peru, Illinois 61354

Ebony Jr! (ages 6–12)
820 S. Michigan Avenue
Chicago, Illinois 60605

Flying Pencil Press (ages 8–14)
P.O. Box 7667
Elgin, Illinois 60121

Highlights for Children (ages 2–11)
803 Church Street
Honesdale, Pennsylvania 18431

Jack and Jill (ages 8–12)
P.O. Box 567B
Indianapolis, Indiana 46206

Stone Soup (ages 5–14)
P.O. Box 83
Santa Cruz, California 95063

National Written and Illustrated by...
(This is an awards contest for students in all grade levels. Write for rules and guidelines.)
Landmark Editions, Inc.
P.O. Box 4469
Kansas City, Missouri 64127

Glossary

absolute location—See exact location.

altiplano—a high plateau or valley between higher mountains; particularly the high plain where the Andes divide in Peru and Bolivia

altitude—the height of land above the level of the sea

Antarctic Circle—an imaginary circle parallel to the equator and 23 degrees 30' from the South Pole.

aquifer—an underground reservoir of water contained within a porous rock layer

archipelago—a group or chain of islands

Arctic Circle—an imaginary circle parallel to the equator and 23 degrees 30' from the North Pole.

atoll—a ring of coral islands encircling a lagoon

axis—an imaginary line that runs through the center of the Earth from the North Pole to the South Pole

basin—an area of land that is surrounded by higher land

bay—a body of water having land on at least two sides

boundary—a line on a map that separates one country from another

canal—a waterway dug across land for ships to go through

canyon—a deep valley with steep sides

cape—a piece of land that extends into a river, lake, or ocean

cardinal directions—the four main points of the compass: north, south, east, and west

cargo—a load of products carried from one place to another

cartographer—a map maker

channel—a waterway between two land masses; also, the part of a river that is deepest and carries the most water

climate—the kind of weather a region has over a long period of time

communication—the sending out of ideas and information; the means by which people do this

compass rose—the drawing that shows the directions of north, south, east, and west on a map

conservation—preserving valuable resources

continent—one of the seven main land masses on the earth's surface: North America, South America, Europe, Asia, Africa, Australia, and Antarctica

continental divide—the geographic area that separates the direction in which water currents flow

continental shelf—the shallow, gently sloping sea floor that surrounds each continent

Glossary (cont.)

country—the territory of a nation, marked by a boundary that separates it from other nations

current—a fast-moving stream of water in the ocean

degree—one 360th part of the circumference of a circle; used as a unit of measurement

delta—an area of silt, sand, and gravel deposited at the mouth of a river

deposit—a large area of mineral deep in the Earth

desert—a very dry area of land covered with rocks and/or sand

distance scale—a measuring line on a map that helps to figure out the distance from one place to another

dormant volcano—a temporarily inactive volcano

drought—a long period without rain

economic activity—a way that people use their resources to live

ecosystem—a system formed by the interaction of living organisms with each other and with their environment

environment—the surroundings in which everything lives

equator—the imaginary line that circles the middle of the earth, halfway between the North Pole and the South Pole

erosion—the wearing away of land by the elements (ice, sun, water, and wind)

escarpment—a cliff separating two nearly flat land surfaces that lie at different levels

estuary—the widening mouth of a river where it meets the sea; tides ebb and flow within this area

exact location—the location of a point which can be given in latitude and longitude, also called absolute location

extinct volcano—a totally inactive volcano

fertile—good for growing plants and crops

fjord—a narrow, steep-sided ocean inlet that reaches far into a coastline

forest—a large area covered with trees and undergrowth

frontier—land that is mostly unsettled

geothermal power—energy from heat within the Earth

geyser—a hot spring that shoots water and steam into the air

Glossary *(cont.)*

glacier—a large, thick, slow moving mass of ice

globe—a round model of the Earth

gorge—a deep, narrow passage between mountains

grassland—a wide area covered with grass and an occasional tree

grid—a series of evenly spaced lines used to locate places on a map

grove—a large field of trees

growing season—the period of time in which the weather is warm enough for crops to grow

gulf—an area of sea that is partly surrounded by land

---

harbor—a body of water sheltered by natural or artificial barriers and deep enough to moor ships

hemisphere—half of a sphere; on a globe, a hemisphere represents one half of the Earth

highland—an area of hills or mountains

humid—moist or damp

hurricane—a fierce storm of wind and rain

hydroelectric power—electric energy produced by water power

---

iceberg—a huge chunk of ice floating in the sea

ice sheet—a broad, thick layer of glacial ice that covers a wide area

irrigation—supplying water to dry land through pipes, ditches, or canals

island—a piece of land entirely surrounded by water

isthmus—a narrow strip of land that connects two larger landmasses and has water on both sides

---

jungle—a hot, humid area of land which is overgrown with trees and other plants

---

key—the section that explains the symbols used on a map

---

lagoon—a shallow body of water that opens on the sea but is protected by a sandbar or coral reef

lake—a body of water completely surrounded by land

landform—a shape of land, such as a mountain, valley, or plateau

Glossary (cont.)

landforms map—a map that uses colors to show the height and shape of the land; also called a contour map

landlocked country—a country surrounded by land without access to the sea

landmark—an important thing or place that stands out from everything around it

latitude line—an east-west line drawn parallel to the equator on a globe

lava—hot, liquid rock

location—the position of a point on the surface of the earth; can be exact or relative

longitude line—a north-south line drawn from pole to pole on a globe

lowland—a low, flat area of land

manufacturing—making finished goods from raw materials

map—a drawing of all or part of the earth's surface showing where things are located

meridian—any of the lines of longitude running north and south on a globe or map and representing a great circle of the Earth that passes through the poles

mesa—a broad, flat-topped landform with steep sides found in arid or semiarid regions

mineral—a natural occurring substance found on the earth

mining—the process of taking mineral deposits from the earth

moisture—water or other liquids in the air or on the ground; wetness

monsoon—a wind that produces wet and dry seasons in southern and eastern Asia

moor—an open expanse of rolling land covered with grass or other low vegetation

moraine—an accumulation of debris carried and deposited by a glacier

mountain—a large mass of land that rises high above the surrounding land

mountain range—a group or series of mountains

mouth—the place where a river empties into a larger body of water

natural gas—a light mineral often used for fuel; usually found near petroleum

natural resource—something occurring in nature that people need or want

North Pole—the point located at the most northern place on a globe

oasis—a place in the desert where water from underground springs allows plants to grow

ocean—a large body of salt water that covers much of the earth's surface

ore—a mixture of rock, soil, and minerals

outback—the remote backcountry of Australia

Glossary *(cont.)*

parallel—any of the imaginary lines parallel to the equator and representing degrees of latitude on the Earth's surface

peninsula—a body of land almost completely surrounded by water

petroleum—an oily liquid mineral

place—an area having characteristics that define them and make them different from other areas

plain—a low, flat land area

plateau—an area of flat land higher than the land around it

pollution—damage to air, water, or land by smoke, dust, or chemicals

population—all of the people who live in a particular place

population density—the number of people living in each square mile or kilometer of an area

port—a place where ships can load

prairie—a large area of flat land covered with tall, thick grass

preservation—keeping things safe from damage or destruction

prime meridian (Greenwich Meridian)—the special longitude line that is the starting point for measuring all the other lines of longitude

projection—a way of transferring the features of the Earth as represented on a globe to a flat piece of paper (map); the resulting style of map

rain forest—dense forest mostly composed of broadleaved evergreens found in wet tropical regions

ravine—a narrow valley with steep sides

raw material—a material in its natural state, used for making finished goods

reef—a narrow ridge of rock, sand, or coral just above or below the surface of the water

region—an area having distinctive characteristics that make it different from the surrounding areas

relative location—the location of a point on the earth's surface in relation to other points

reservoir—a lake or pond where water is stored for future use

resource—a supply of valuable or useful things such as water, coal, soil, forests, or air; see natural resource

revolution—the movement of the Earth in orbit around the sun; one complete revolution equals a year

river—a large stream of water flowing in a channel

rotation—the movement of the earth turning on its axis; one complete rotation equals 24 hours

rural—away from cities and close to farms

Glossary (cont.)

savanna—a tropical grassland with scattered trees

scale—the ratio of map distance to actual distance on the Earth's surface

sea—a large body of salt water

sound—a long, broad ocean inlet usually parallel to the coast, or a long stretch of water separating an island from the mainland

South Pole—the point located at the most southern place on a globe

state—the strongest governing body, subordinate to a national government (Not to be confused with the nation-state.)

steppe—a grassland in the temperate zone where limited rainfall prevents tree growth

strait—a narrow waterway that connects two seas

swamp—a lowland area covered with shallow water and dense vegetation

symbol—something that stands for a real thing

temperature—the measure of how hot or cold a place is

territory—a region that is owned or controlled by another country or political unit

time zone—one of 24 areas or zones of the Earth in which the time is one hour earlier than in the zone to its east

tributary—a river or stream that flows into a larger body of water

transportation—the way in which people or goods travel or are moved from one place to another

Tropic of Cancer—the parallel of latitude that lies 23 degrees 27' north of the equator

Tropic of Capricorn—the parallel of latitude that lies 23 degrees 27' south of the equator

tundra—a wide, treeless arctic plain where few plants or animals live because of frozen subsoil called permafrost

urban sea—the city and its surrounding built-up area

valley—a long, low area between hills or mountains

volcano—an opening in the earth's surface through which hot liquid rock (magma) and other materials are forced out

weather—the condition of the air at a certain time or place

Software Review

Software: *From Alice to Ocean: Alone Across the Outback* (Claris)

Hardware: Macintosh computer (4MB) and CD-ROM player

Grade Level: Intermediate Level

Summary: *From Alice to Ocean: Alone Across the Outback*, allows your students to follow Robyn Davidson's 1,700 mile (2,720 km) trek across the Australian outback. She makes her journey with her dog and four camels. The adventure is narrated by Robyn and documented by a National Geographic photographer. Included in the program software is an on-screen map to allow students to track Robyn's progress across the outback. The software also includes text on plant and animal life, aboriginal culture, the environment, etc. Using this program your students will have the opportunity to experience the Australian outback without having to really be there.

Bibliography

Arnold, Caroline. *A Walk on the Great Barrier Reef.* Carolrhoda, 1988.

Baillie, Allan. *Adrift.* Viking, 1992.

Baker, Jeannie. *Where the Forest Meets the Sea.* Greenwillow, 1988.

Browne, Rolle. *A Family in Australia.* Lerner, 1987.

Browne, Rolle. *An Aboriginal Family.* Lerner, 1985.

Crossland, Bert. *Where on Earth Are We?* Book Links. September, 1994.

Czernecki, Stefan, and Timothy Rhodes. *The Singing Snake.* Hyperion, 1993.

Dickinson, Mary B (Ed.) *National Geographic Picture Atlas of Our World.* National Geographic Society, 1993.

Dolce, Laura. *Australia.* Chelsea, 1990.

Fatchen, Max. *The Country Mail Is Coming: Poems from Down Under.* Little, 1990.

Fox, Mary B. *New Zealand.* Childrens, 1991.

Garret, Dan. *Australia.* Raintree, 1990.

Geographic Education National Implementation Project. Guidelines, 1987.

Germaine, Elizabeth, and Ann L. Burckhardt. *Cooking the Australian Way.* Lerner, 1990.

Gittins, Anne. *Tales from the South Pacific Islands.* Stemmer, 1977.

Gleeson, Libby. *Eleanor, Elizabeth.* Holiday, 1990.

Gleitzman, Morris. *Misery Guts*. Harcourt, 1993.

Kelleher, Victor. *Bailey's Bones.* Dial, 1989.

Kelly, Andrew. *Australia.* Watts, 1989.

Keyworth, Valerie. *New Zealand: Land of the Long White Cloud.* Macmillan, 1990.

Klwin, Robin. *All in the Blue Clouded Weather.* Viking, 1992.

Lepthien, Emilie U. *Australia.* Childrens, 1982.

Lepthien, Emilie U. *The Philippines.* Childrens, 1986.

Margolies, Barbara A. *Warriors, Wigmen, and the Crocodile People: Journeys in Papua New Guinea.* Macmillan, 1993.

Nance, John. *Lobo of the Tasaday: A Stone Age Boy Meets the Modern World.* Pantheon, 1982.

Reynolds, Jan. *Down Under: Vanishing Cultures.* Harcourt, 1992.

Scholes, Katherine. *The Landing: A Night of Birds.* Doubleday, 1990.

Te Kanawa, Kiri. *Land of the Long White Cloud: Maori Myths, Tales, and Legends.* Arcade, 1990.

Thiele, Colin. *Shadow Shark.* Harper, 1988.

Thiele, Colin. *Storm Boy.* Harper, 1978.

Topek, Lily R. *Philippines.* Marshall Cavendish, 1991.

Trezise, Percy, and Dick Roughsey. *Turramulh the Giant Quinkin.* Stevens, 1988.

Wheatley, Nadia. *My Place.* Kane-Miller, 1992.

Wiremu, Graham. *The Maoris of New Zealand.* Rourke, 1987.

Wrightson, Patricia. *Moon-Dark.* Macmillan, 1988.

Bibliography *(cont.)*

Technology

Broderbund. ***MacGlobe & PC Globe.*** Available from Learning Services, (800)877-9378. disk

Broderbund. ***Where in the World Is Carmen Sandiego?*** Available from Troll, (800)526-5289. CD-ROM and disk

Bureau of Electronic Publishing Inc. ***World Fact Book.*** Available from Educational Resources, (800)624-2926. CD-ROM

Claris Corporation. ***From Alice to Ocean: Alone Across the Outback.*** Available from Educational Resources, (800)624-2926. CD-ROM

CLEARVUE. ***The Earth, the Oceans, and Plants & Animals:*** Interactive, curriculum oriented CD-ROMs. Available from Educational Resources, (800)624-2926. CD-ROM

DeLorme Publishing. ***Global Explorer.*** Available from DeLorme Publishing, 1995. CD-ROM

Impressions, My First World Atlas. Available from Educational Resources, (800)624-2926.

Lawrence. ***Nigel's World Adventures in World Geography.*** Available from Educational Resources, (800)624-2926. CD-ROM and disk

Learningways, Inc. ***Explore-Australia.*** Available from William K. Bradford Publishing Co., (800)421-2009. disk

Magic Quest. ***Time Treks and Earth Treks.*** Available from Educational Resources, (800)624-2926. disk, CD-ROM, and laserdisc

MECC. ***Odell Down Under.*** Available from MECC, (800)685-MECC. disk.

MECC. ***World GeoGraph.*** Available from Educational Resources, (800)624-2926. disk

Mindscape. ***World Atlas.*** Available from Educational Resources, (800)624-2926. disk

National Geographic. ***STV: World Geography.*** Available from National Geographic Educational Technology, (800)328-2936. videodisc

National Geographic. ***Zip Zap Map.*** Available from Educational Resources, (800)624-2926. laserdisc and disk

Newton Technology. ***GEOvista Tutor.*** Available from William K. Bradford, (800)421-2009. disk

Orange Cherry. ***Time Traveler.*** Available from Educational Resources, (800)624-2926. CD-ROM

Pride in Learning. ***Global Issues.*** Available from Educational Resources, (800)624-2926. disk

Queue. ***Atlas Explorer.*** Available from Educational Resources, (800)624-2926. disk

Sanctuary Woods. ***Ecology Treks.*** Available from Learning Services, (800)624-2926. software and videodisc

Software Toolworks. ***World Atlas.*** Available from Learning Services, (800)877-9378. CD-ROM and disk

SVE. ***Geography on Laserdisc.*** Available from Learning Services, (800)877-9378. laserdisc.

Answer Key

Page 15

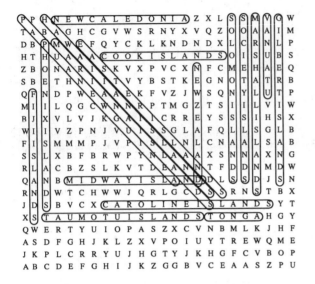

Page 26

1. marsupial
2. koala
3. eucalyptus
4. kangaroo
5. wallaby
6. wombat
7. dugong
8. platypus
9. emu
10. echidna
11. skink
12. dingo
13. cassowary
14. kookaburra
15. bandicoots
16. lyrebird
17. Tasmanian devil
18. weaverbird

Pages 44–45

1. an island built from the skeletons of coral polyps
2. 1,250 miles (2,000 km)
3. in the Coral Sea off the northeast coast of Australia
4. tiny coral polyps
5. millions of years
6. about 1,500 species
7. about 400 kinds
8. rose coral

   brain coral

   mushroom coral

   fan coral
9. between 10 miles (16 km) and 150 miles (190 km) from the shore
10. answers will vary